Self Induced Mind Control

By Gregory T. Peele

Table of Contents

Introduction

Have you ever heard of self-induced mind control?

Mind control strikes fear in a lot of people. The term conjures images of old movies, where evil hypnotists convert innocent people into zombie killers with the ding of a bell or some other trigger. There are also terrifying rumors of the Nazis, the Soviet Union, the CIA, and other government groups conducting inhumane mind control experiments on unwilling victims, often with sinister results.

But do not be afraid. Self-induced mind control is not like the mind control of the movies. Rather, it could be the best thing that you ever do for yourself. The great thing about self-induced mind control is that you become your own master, far more than you are now. There are no limits in what you can do once you master control over your mind.

You may think that you are already in control of your own mind. It is your mind, after all, right? You may think that you are aware of and in control of everything you think and everything you believe.

But have you noticed that some areas of your life are lacking? Have you noticed that no matter how hard you try, some things just don't ever work out for you? Despite your best efforts, do you encounter hurdles with weight loss, meeting a romantic partner, resolving family conflicts, or getting a promotion at work? And, last but not least, do you find yourself constantly worrying or thinking about things that you don't want to think about? Does it seem like your thoughts are just out of control, whizzing at you from nowhere, when you least expect it or need it?

These things are all indicative that you do not have the control over your own mind that you think you have. You have negative thoughts and self-effacing beliefs that are limiting you from success. And you let these thoughts and beliefs limit you, because you are not able to control them.

It is possible that these beliefs and thoughts were introduced to you from an early age and now they seem to be an integral part of who you are, to the point that you are so used to them that you are unaware of them. It is also possible that these thoughts have been placed into your mind by the trauma and disappointments that naturally arise in life. No matter why those thoughts are nestled in your brain, there is no need to hang onto them. They are only hurting you. It is crucial to let them go and move on with better thoughts that do not hinder your success in life. This is where you can use self-induced mind control for your advantage.

There is probably something in your life that you want to change. Something that you want to be successful in. What is that? It could be one thing, or many things. It could do with improving yourself, or just your situation in life. Find what you really want to be successful in.

Then find what is holding you back. Do you have some sort of belief that you are not good enough and will never succeed? Do you think that you are powerless? Perhaps you believe that it is unattainable to reach your goals because of money, which may relate to an even deeper belief within your mind that you are not good enough to make big money.

Whatever your goals are, they are attainable. And whatever is holding you back mentally is probably just a belief or negative thought that you are not in control over. Gaining control of your own mind is basically you handing the reigns to yourself; you are taking control of your mind and thus of your life. You are thinking better thoughts, letting go of negative thought patterns that cause you distress and limit your success, and you are feeling both more satisfied with your life and more in control. You will begin to realize that your thoughts dramatically affect what happens to you, and that self-induced mind control can help you keep your life positive and free of the stressors and hurdles that keep you down right now.

In this book, you will learn to identify some of the thoughts and beliefs that are limiting your success. Then you will learn ways to gain control over your own mind so that you can alter your thoughts into more positive and helpful ones. Use this book as a guide to get started on a journey of self-induced mind control that can totally transform your life. This book is just an inspiration; there is so much more you can achieve with your mind if you begin working on it.

This book is not a magical cure for all that is wrong in your life. It will not be an easy fix to anything. Self-induced mind control itself is not an easy task that you can just master in one reading of this book. Rather, it is a journey that requires constant work. But just like working out is worth it in the end when you become healthier and more muscular, so is self-induced mind control when you begin to make healthier choices in life because you believe in your own self-worth and have a consciously positive attitude. This book is your beginning.

Chapter 1: Regulating Your Thoughts

The first and foremost part of self-induced mind control lies in taking control of your thinking. Your thought patterns and your internal beliefs are things that you may think you have control of, but really you don't. Controlling your thoughts can have a dramatic impact on how your life goes for you.

Why is this? What we as humans believe resonates in how we act. What we think manifests in our choices. Even if we don't realize it, subconscious beliefs and negative thoughts patterns dictate everything we do, which in turn influences how our lives go.

Thoughts can easily become habitual. You probably have thoughts patterns and habits that you are not even aware of because you have held them for so long that they feel like an irrevocable and natural part of you. When you understand that these are simply habits and not a true part of who you are, then you can begin to break the habits. First it is important to identify these habits.

Old habits die hard, they say, and this is true even for thought patterns. Yes, it is hard to break mental habits that you have held for years. But once you identify the habit, you begin to build awareness of it. Then you begin to think of ways to break it. Identifying harmful thought patterns is an important first step in overcoming these habits. It builds a personal awareness that can inspire you to bring about change and to realize what you are thinking, so that you can recognize bad thoughts in the future and change them. It seems hard at first, but becomes surprisingly easy as time goes on and you gain awareness and practice in regulating your thoughts.

First, what comes to mind first when you hear good news? Do you think, "Oh, great, something good is happening to me; what will life do to take this good thing away from me?" Or "Oh, great, how will I screw this one up?" Or "Wow. How did I get this good news? I don't deserve this."

How about when you start a new diet? Is there some part of you, under the enthusiasm and certainty that you will stick with it this time, that chimes in, "You probably won't stick this one out either"?

Or when somebody asks you out, do you feel like you are scared? Is there some part of you that thinks this will fall apart, like all your past relationships? That you will do something to screw it up, or that he/she is probably a psycho because you only attract psychos?

Think about it for a while. Be honest with yourself. If you encounter hurdles or unexplainable repeat problems in your life, there is likely a negative thought at the root of it. You may not be aware of that thought at first, but a careful and brutally honest review of your original first thoughts in reaction to events in your life can help unveil what this thought is. This thought usually pops up first thing, and creates a sinking feeling in your gut as it tugs down your optimism. But then you bury it under fake happiness, or rationale. Or perhaps you bury yourself in this first thought, never fully realizing just how negative and hopeless you are being.

These first thoughts may be fleeting or they may be so common that they seem totally normal. So it may not seem that they matter. But they do, more than you know. Your underlying thought habits, the things that you think about first, say a lot about your mental state and what you are unconsciously putting out into the world with your actions.

Your main hurdling thought habit may also be something that you obsess over so much that you are used to it. Consider things you think about all the time. Do you constantly think about past failed relationships, a traumatic past event, a mortifying event at work, or a missed opportunity? Do you constantly worry about future tragedy or screwing up a project? The things you think about the most can reflect what bothers you to your core and can indicate underlying beliefs that cause you to act in ways that continue to hurt your ability to be successful.

When you identify the bad thought habit you have, dig a little deeper. What does this negative thought pattern say about yourself? It likely reveals a self-belief you hold deep within your mind. These beliefs are different for everybody, but consider these common self-limiting beliefs that cause negative thought patterns.

Fear of a new relationship or dread of a promotion at work can indicate that you do not believe you are good enough. In fact, most likely, all your negative thoughts come from a belief that you are not good enough. This may stem from your childhood, when family intentionally or unintentionally reinforced the belief. Then it has likely become reaffirmed over the years by romantic rejections, being overlooked at work, or colossal mistakes that you made with money, friends, family, drugs, sex, you name it.

But even mistakes in the past or the hurtful beliefs of others does not mean that you aren't good enough for success. You must identify this self-effacing belief, and kill it! You are good enough. Stop worrying if you are good enough for anyone else; you never will meet everyone's expectations. What's important is that you are good enough for you. Only you can believe in yourself, so start now. If you believe in yourself, you will be shocked at how "good enough" you become.

It's also possible that your negative thoughts arise from a past trauma. Something tragic in your past makes you believe that anything good that happens to you is likely to be taken away or to not be as good as it seems. It can be hard to trust that life has anything good to offer you, especially after you have been through the worst possible. Tragedies can and do happen all the time. Maybe you were a victim of assault, abuse, or a crime, or you lost a loved one who was very dear to you, or life just seems to keep tearing you down whenever you finally attain some semblance of peace. These are all possible traumas that can impact your thoughts very profoundly.

But you must understand that just because a tragedy has happened to you, does not mean that the rest of your life is going to be tragic. There is the possibility for good as much as there is for bad. Feeling optimistic can feel better than worrying all the time, so embrace positivity. Either way, your thoughts cannot necessarily prevent tragedy, so why spend all your time shutting out the good things and the good thoughts in anticipation of something terrible that you cannot prevent anyway? Often worrying about tragedy invites it and sets up your life for it. Conversely, positivity can invite more positive experiences into your life. Enjoy your time on Earth instead with positive thinking. In the end, you will be surprised how good things will come to you if you anticipate them and work toward them mentally.

You may also have a habit of blaming others for messing things up for you. This thought habit can arise from an internal belief that no one is up to any good, and everyone has it out for you. Your habit of blaming keeps you from accepting the good in others and feeling joyful about new relationships or new opportunities. You harbor a sense of bitterness, as if the world owes you something.

Sadly, this is not true. The world owes you nothing; you have to work for what you want, and be a go-getter. What happens to you is not necessarily your fault, but sometimes it is. You need to quit relying on others to affirm who you are and what happens in your life. Rather, take responsibility for life and begin believing in yourself. If you do things yourself, you won't be disappointed by others.

There are many other possible self-effacing beliefs that may underlie your thinking. Find what makes sense to you. Write it down if you have to, or talk to someone close to you. Talk to a counselor. Meditate. Do whatever helps you get in tune with your thoughts, your past, and your internal beliefs. This is a time to be brutally honest.

The identification process is not always a pleasant or easy one. But it is Step One in regulating your thoughts, which is the main purpose of self-induced mind control. To gain control of the problem, one generally has to understand the problem. So figure out your own mind. Then you can begin to take control of it.

Make a commitment to yourself, to your future, to your loved ones: You will learn to regulate your thoughts. You will DO THIS. Once you commit to it and learn your own mind, you can begin the process of creating new thinking habits. Out with the old negative thoughts; in with new, positive thoughts.

Once you know what thoughts are hurting you, and probably hindering your success in life, now you can begin choosing better thoughts. If you think you're not good enough, make a commitment to thinking that you are. If you blame the world or others for everything, make a commitment to not thinking of others but rather of yourself and your own abilities. If you fear that all good things will be taken away, make a commitment to believing that something good will come out of life and every day is a chance for something good to happen to you.

Pick your new thought habits. Pick the ways you want to see the world. It can be as unrealistic and optimistic as you like. This is not about being realistic; it is about being positive and happy with the way your own mind is working.

Then, you can begin the process of regulating your own thoughts!

It will take a conscious effort. But when something happens and the familiar old negative thought pops into your head, immediately think your new, more positive thought. Redirect your mind away from the thoughts you want to change, and onto the thoughts you want to fill your mind with.

Some physical reminders may be helpful in redirecting your mind. When you begin to obsess over familiar worries or insecurities, choose to rub your hands together, or to focus on your breath. This takes your mind off of your thoughts and puts them on something physical.

Also try to set aside a few hours a week for actual meditation. Meditation may sound silly and New Age-y, but it's actually an excellent way to get to know your own mind and gain mind control. Meditate on positive things, so that your mind gets used to thinking about them. This is your way of introducing the positive thoughts you wish to think to your mind so that they can become a part of your regular thought patterns.

Never underestimate the power of affirmations, as well. Verbal or mental affirmations are incredibly powerful ways to cement new beliefs into your mental thinking habits. Out loud or in your mind, repeat mantras that enforce the beliefs you wish to accept in your mind. Choose mantras that speak to you and make you feel good. They can be silly, or serious. "I am a good person." "I do deserve the best." "I will succeed at this." "I am beautiful, inside and out." Affirm what it is that you want to believe about yourself, and your mind will eventually accept it as a reality.

It is not easy at first, but you will be surprised at how quickly your mind will accept new thinking habits with just a little time and determination. With practice, your mind will begin to use the positive thoughts first, rather than the old negative ones that hurt you. Then a new and better thought pattern will become established as your way of thinking.

Thinking more positively can have countless benefits from the very start. Even if you have to force it and don't really believe your optimistic thoughts, just thinking them can help release serotonin and dopamine in your brain, neurochemicals that make you feel good. Who doesn't want to feel better?

And you might actually smile at these thoughts. A smile also releases serotonin. It makes you look more inviting to other people, opening better personal connections. It can even make you more attractive to yourself, boosting your self-esteem.

As you start to feel better and start to change your thinking habits, you begin to put out more positive energy. You make more of an effort at work or in your marriage or at the gym, in whatever you are struggling with. You try things you never did before, just because they might be good for you. When you begin to see success and joy in your life because you are making a different effort, then you begin to actually believe your forced beliefs. They become affirmed, and hence they become real. They are cemented in your mind as a reality and thus they can become a habit that your mind accepts.

Chapter 2: Regulate Your Life

Changing your thoughts will change your life in many powerful and major ways. But changing your life can help you change your thoughts. The two can work hand in hand when you are trying to bring about positive transformation. It's a cycle.

You can't expect life to just get better if you continue to hold onto the same patterns, bad habits, and bad friends as always. Your life is a reflection of your beliefs about yourself. All your behaviors and habits suggest something that you secretly believe is true about yourself.

If you smoke or use drugs, it is likely because you don't care about yourself and don't feel good enough to bother maintaining your health. If you have bad friends, it's likely because you don't believe you are worth any better. If you gossip and cause drama at work, you are only hurting your chances of going farther in your field, your bad behavior reflects your belief that you are not a better person than that.

Part of regulating your thoughts includes regulating your life. Make the changes that you want to see. Find what in your life continues to reinforce and reflect your bad thought patterns. The "trash" in your life may be friends, family, co-workers, bad health habits, an ugly home, poor spending and budgeting habits, or sloppy work habits. Just having a messy room or an unflattering wardrobe can have significant negative effects on your mental state, because they reflect to you that you are not good enough and you cannot do better.

Regulating your life is potentially the hardest part of this whole self-induced mind control process. But it is so important. It is not a step that you can just skip. If you want true transformation, you better be active in performing it. Only you can bring about control of your life and that means that you must take control.

Some changes are not realistic right away. It is never easy to just turn your back on family, nor is it necessarily the best idea. It may not feasible to just upgrade your job, your home, or your wardrobe overnight in your current financial situation. But you can make small adjustments that can have profound impacts in the long run.

For instance, start making an effort with your appearance. Even if you can't afford a new wardrobe, you can add some changes to your look. Try new color combinations and add belts and cheap accessories to look your best. Start working out at home if you can't afford a gym. There are free Youtube workout videos. Avoid certain conversations with your family that are hurtful. Clean up your messy home. Fix broken furniture, or repaint your bathroom.

It doesn't have to be a huge change to be significant. Even the tiniest of changes can indicate to yourself that you are making an effort. This can help your mind accept the fact that changes are coming. It can also help you feel better about yourself, as you use your abilities to repair your life and move it in a positive direction.

Just baby steps are sometimes all we are ready to take. That's OK. Everyone has to start somewhere. But at least make those baby steps. Doing nothing will result in nothing.

The best first baby step is recognizing and clarifying your true goals. Maybe you know exactly what they are. Maybe you have no clue. Sit down with a notebook and draw or write your goals. Putting them on paper can make them more tangible. At this point in time, there is no need for a plan; plans will come to you when you are ready and have enough control over your mind to make good ones that are truly attainable. Just actualize your goals in life.

Being aware of your own goals can help set them in motion. You begin to think about them. You begin to do little things, taking more baby steps in the direction of your final intended journey.

Most importantly, set aside some "you" time. This is a huge baby step in the direction of goal completion. Taking some time for yourself indicates to your mind that you are worth something and that you are deserving of care. This can help your mind begin to build self-esteem and can help affirm your new positive self-beliefs.

Whether you dedicate this time to pedicures or a hobby or simple meditation, there is no right or wrong way to spend "you" time. It is just important to take time to care for yourself and your own needs. Don't worry about your responsibilities to other people, your problems, or even the ways you need to improve yourself. You have plenty of time to worry about these things at other times, so clear them from your mind for a little while each week and just focus on enjoying an activity that is dear to you.

Elevate your life. This is especially important to elevating yourself and your situation to a better plane of existence. As your thoughts begin to become more positive, so must your life. Wherever you see an opportunity for improvement, make it. Surround yourself with people that live life the way you want to live it. Cut bad habits and adopt good ones.

An elevated life will in turn elevate you. This is the practical application of mind control and it is very important. It isn't about deserving change. Put the notion of deserving things or not deserving them out of your mind. Rather, it is about needing change to improve your mental state and achieve self-induced mind control.

Again, it's far from easy. But it is so worth it.

Chapter 3: Self-Hypnosis

A major tool in self-induced mind control is self-hypnosis. Self-hypnosis is often compared to putting yourself into a trance. Imagine attaining total physical relaxation, and total awareness of everything going on within your mind. Then imagine being able to accept all your thoughts, even the disturbing ones, and then redirect them into nicer thoughts.

Basically, this is self-induced mind control. It is total control of your mind. However, it is a little bit different. That's because self-hypnosis requires total focus and concentration on your own mind. It is not practical to use self-hypnosis all the time. You couldn't work, clean your house, or anything else if you were constantly in self-hypnosis.

Rather, self-hypnosis is a useful tool that can help you get used to having control over your own mind. It can get you accustomed to having self-induced mind control, so that you can begin to practice the mind control all the time, even when fully conscious and not under hypnosis.

Don't let the term "hypnosis" scare you. You won't turn into a mindless zombie with no self-control. If anything, you will gain better control over yourself. Self-hypnosis is not scary because you are performing it on yourself. You can stop the process if you get uncomfortable. You can also use it to explore it your own mind without inhibition and without the judgment of another person. Basically, self-hypnosis is your chance to spend time with yourself and be uniquely you.

Hypnosis has been associated with healing. This is your opportunity to heal yourself mentally, in a sense. All of this journey is about taking control of your mind; and in this case, you are taking control of your own healing. Let that thought give you a rich sense of accomplishment and reward. How many people get to heal themselves? That is a tremendous accomplishment.

Self-hypnosis should feel healing, never unpleasant or horrible. There may be moments of discomfort as you encounter ugly thoughts in the peace of your mind, but self-hypnosis instructs you to accept those thoughts without a fight and then turn your focus back to your breathing, or a sound you have chosen to fixate on.

There are a variety of self-hypnosis methods. No two are the same. You must find what works for you. In time, you may even develop your own special journey into the hypnotic state. The greatest thing about self-hypnosis is that it is actually a natural state of mind, so achieving it is something that can come to you naturally.

Steps to Self-Hypnosis

To begin self-hypnosis, you first need to be in a comfortable environment. Put on comfortable clothes. Be in a room that you feel safe in. Make sure you will not be disturbed by turning off your phone, locking the door, putting pets outside, arranging for your kids to be busy, etc. Some people like to do this while lying in bed, waiting for sleep; others like to do it mid-day, perhaps during a dead time in the office, or when home alone. Some like to hike out to a special spot in the woods or on the coast. Find your real-life happy place.

Next, sit or lie down on a comfortable piece of furniture or even the ground. Make sure that it is comfortable. There is nothing worse than an uncomfortable bump on the ground digging into your shoulder blade and interrupting your peaceful trance.

Now, determine your goal for this hypnosis. What do you hope to focus on accomplishing? There are no limits. For the purposes of this book, the goal is to gain control over your mind. But you can actually use self-hypnosis to gain mind control and enable yourself to tackle a specific goal, such as quitting smoking or losing weight. So what really needs to be improved in your life? Spend this time achieving what you really need to achieve. This is all about improving your life and being successful, so don't limit yourself.

Using the goal you choose, create a specific affirmation. "I choose to stop smoking. Cigarettes are nasty and I don't crave nicotine at all." "I am losing weight. My clothes are already a size smaller." "I have more energy. I feel like I am actually alive. I am no longer depressed." These are just examples; create your own mantra that feels good and actually convinces you that you are achieving your goal.

Now it's time to "go under." Don't feel fearful; this is the best part, when you get to relax. Choose a point in the room to focus on. Never take your eyes off of it. Begin to focus on your breathing. Breathe in, breathe out. Try to let go of all thoughts and all emotions. This may not always be easy. Especially if you have poor mind control, you might have constant intruding thoughts and worries. Don't follow them but don't fight them either. Just accept the thought, think it in full, then return to focusing on the point in the room and your breath.

At this point, when you have gained some focus, you can start paying attention to your body. There are spots where you hold tension. These spots could be in your toes, in your shoulders, in the skin on your forehead.

Wherever it is, touch each part of your body with your mind and force it to relax. That tension is not serving anyone; let it go. It is easiest to follow a pattern, so that you don't miss any spots. Start with your right thumb, circle up your arm, over your head, down your right leg, up your left leg, through the left side of your head, and down your left arm, ending in your left thumb.

This the part where you can get creative. You are now deeply relaxed. So try to feel that relaxation. It should feel like you are floating. Imagine that you are submerged in water, or floating on a feather in the sky, or drifting through Outer Space. Whatever makes you happy and relaxes you further. You don't want to imagine you are submerged in water if you are scared of drowning, for instance. This is your time and your space so don't let anyone tell you what to do. Create the hypnotic state that is the best for you.

While relaxed, you are in an impressionable state. You can start to repeat your previously chosen mantra. Your mind will more easily accept the mantra as truth when you are in this highly relaxed and hypnotized state. As your mind accepts the mantra, it begins to think it's true. Thus, you program your mind to take action toward the goal that you have been speaking into existence with your affirmation, or mantra.

Finally, when you feel ready, begin to exit your hypnotic state. You can envision yourself taking steps out of the water, or drifting back down to Earth from the sky or Space. Consciously drive yourself back into awareness and reality. Once you are back in reality, take a few breaths until you are ready to open your eyes.

You may feel a bit strange, especially if this is your first time. It is a bit disorienting to descend into deep relaxation and then ascend back into reality. This is totally normal. Even if it is unpleasant, it will get easier with time.

This exciting form of hypnosis is so easy. You can do it all by yourself. And you can reap so many benefits from it.

Chapter 4: Meditation

Meditation is another way to get in touch with your inner mind for a while. There are multiple ways that you can meditate. Each form of meditation is different, but equally helpful. Try different meditations to find what you like the best.

Mindfulness Meditation

Mindfulness meditation is a great way to get the mental awareness of the present necessary for mind control. With mindfulness meditation, you can learn to be aware of your surroundings, which aids in identifying harmful thoughts and regulating them with positive thoughts, the key to self-induced mind control. It is great practice for reshaping how you look at the world and taking control of your mind.

Mindfulness is basically being mindful of your present state. You are aware of everything going on at the current moment, the feeling of the air, the color of the walls, the sounds going on around you, your heart rate, your breathing.

Here are a few simple mindfulness meditations that you can try on your own. These exercises serve more as an introduction to mindfulness meditation than anything. With these meditations, you can determine if mindfulness works for you. You can customize these meditations and find other mindfulness meditations that will achieve the same beneficial affects. As you gain practice in staying in the present moment, you can begin to try longer and more advanced meditations. Guided meditations are great, as are meditations you do on your own. Do not be afraid to guide yourself on your own meditations. There are many phone apps and audio files on the Internet that have guided mindfulness meditations.

The first exercise is a great introduction to mindfulness meditation. It literally takes one minute. Look at the clock, note the time, and then dedicate the next sixty seconds of your life to breathing in and out. This may sound like the self-hypnosis we talked about earlier. That's because mindfulness has many of the same elements as self-hypnosis. But they are different because you are just focusing on your breathing, not on repeating any mantras or affirmations. It is a time to clear your mind and fixate on two things, your inhalations and exhalations.

Another simple exercise is to spend sixty seconds fixating on what you are currently doing. For instance, if you are washing dishes, take some time to focus intently on the feeling of the soap bubbles on your hands, the slipperiness of the porcelain under your fingers, the smell of the detergent. Focus on dishes and only dishes. Or, if you are driving, begin to hyper focus on the feeling of the tires on the asphalt, the smell of your car, and the sound of the engine. Basically, spend a minute tuning out everything but the very present. Don't chase any thoughts in your mind. Don't let worries intrude on your mindfulness. Just focus on the present and be devoid of all thoughts and emotions.

A third exercise may sound silly but it is an incredibly effective way to draw your focus onto the present. This exercise is known as the ten-count. Basically, count to ten. Then count backward to one. Do this for one minute. You can count as quickly or slowly as you want, just don't let your attention wander. Focus entirely on counting.

Zen Meditation

Zen meditation may be the most well-known form of meditation. Zen meditation is the cornerstone of Zen Buddhism. But you do not have to be Buddhist to reap its benefits. This meditation involves sitting still and clearing your mind of all clutter.

This meditation starts with a neutral and peaceful setting. Sit in a posture that allows you to relax but also requires you to focus on your body. Usually the Lotus or half-Lotus position is recommended. Lotus involves crossing your legs and tucking your feet inside your knees. If you are too stiff in the legs to sit in Lotus, try kneeling. Keep your eyes open. This helps keep you stay focused on the purpose of your meditation. Breathe only through your nose, never your mouth. Your breaths should be soft and gentle.

Like in mindfulness, your mind must remain focused on your posture and breathing. But you are not just staying mindful of the present moment. Rather, your goal is achieving Zen, a state of mind where your thoughts are clear and you are not preoccupied with anything. Achieving Zen can be hard for inexperienced meditators. It can take some practice to be able to enter this state fully.

Music and chants are often part of Zen meditation. They can help you cleanse your mind of all thoughts and free yourself to a point where all you are focused on is your meditation. Looking up Zen chants can help you achieve the Zen mind state.

Guided Imagery Meditation

Guided imagery meditation may be the very opposite of mindfulness. This is because it takes your attention away from the present and puts it instead on an alternate reality of your own imagining. It is still very helpful, however, as it lets you hone your imagination and train your mind to follow your instruction. It also clears your mind, so you are not preoccupied with your usual worries and insecurities. This meditation is a great way to uncover things about yourself, such as things that scare you or comfort you. It can open doorways to your innermost desires and wants.

If you have seen the movie or read the book *Fight Club*, you may remember the guided imagery meditation where Tyler Durden encounters a penguin that tells him, "Slide." This is an example of the wild things you can come up with during guided imagery meditation. This entire meditation is founded upon your own unique imagination.

Guided imagery meditation is something that you can follow or do yourself. You will basically begin by relaxing. Usually you attain relaxation through breath and even conscious releasing of tension in the muscles of your body, like in self-hypnosis.

When you are relaxed, you then begin imagining yourself on a journey. You could be walking through a forest, or along a shore. You could be flying in the clouds or drifting through galaxies in Outer Space. This is your domain and your mind; do what feels best for you. You may also imagine yourself assuming different forms, such as the form of a spirit animal of your choosing. This is essentially an escape from reality so be as creative as you want.

Concluding the meditation involves bringing yourself back to reality. You can do this by gradually becoming aware of different aspects of reality. Bring your mind to focus on the ticking of a clock, for instance. This can slowly allow you to resume your conscious awareness of reality and come back out of the meditation.

Guided imagery can help you achieve many goals. You can choose to focus on stress relief, pain relief, weight loss, or just controlling your mind better. You can also just use it as a form of escape. This is the form of meditation that is most often used to help cancer patients and other chronic illness sufferers overcome their symptoms and fear of death.

You can make up your own guided imagery meditation. Just choose a place and a form that comforts you. You can also look up audio files and videos on the Internet or on phone apps to guide you through meditation. Some places also offer meditation groups and meetups, where you can meditate with other like-minded people.

Chapter 5: The Benefits

I have already shared many benefits to self-induced mind control. Really, after reading this book, there should be no doubt in your mind about why self-induced mind control is the best thing you can ever do for yourself. From freeing yourself of mental barriers to attaining your goals and dreams, self-induced mind control is a powerful way to take charge and make your life your own. In this chapter, I will go over some of the benefits in more detail. Use this chapter as motivation for seeking self-induced mind control.

Success

Self-induced mind control is your gateway to success in life. They say the sky is the limit, but really your mind is. Therefore, you must use your mind to achieve success and don't bar yourself from anything.

Often we are unsuccessful because of self-beliefs and mental blocks that prevent us from acting in ways that make us truly successful. But mind control enables you to identify and break down these self-beliefs, and replace them with more helpful self-beliefs. In the end, you are able to believe in yourself. You no longer limit yourself or surround yourself with toxicity and negativity that reflect your subconscious lack of confidence.

Self-Esteem and Self-Empowerment

With your greater success in life comes self-esteem. Self-induced mind control lets you get to know yourself. You begin to love yourself more. With this self-love, comes a belief that you can do anything you set your mind to. It also brings a sense of self-forgiveness. You understand your motives for doing things and so you can forgive yourself for even your dumbest mistakes in life.

Now that you love yourself more, you are able to make better decisions. You now look out for your greater good. Better decisions result in better success in life. Your lifestyle and your thinking reflect your self-love.

You also choose better people to surround yourself with, people who treat you with greater respect and support you in your endeavors. You no longer tolerate being put down or abused the way you did when you did not love yourself.

Cleansing Your Life

Part of self-induced mind control involves cleansing your mind and, consequently, your whole life. As you cleanse your thoughts to be more pure and conducive to success, your whole life becomes cleansed. You start making better decisions that result in your greater good. These decisions can include quitting bad habits and ditching toxic people in your life. They can also include adding more value to your life.

Getting Motivated

It is hard to get motivated when you don't think you are capable of achieving your goals. But when you practice self-induced mind control, motivation comes easily. Suddenly, you know you can do what you want to do. There are no longer blocks keeping you from achieving your fullest. As a result, you are suddenly enabled and even passionate about life again. You have automatic self-motivation to achieve your goals.

This passion and motivation only grows as you begin to see the success self-induced mind control brings you. Or rather, that you bring yourself through mind control. As you begin to make life work out for you, you also begin to feel empowered. You see that you can be truly successful for once. This only serves to motivate you more.

Easing Mental Illness

Just because your life is not perfect does not mean you are mentally ill. You can have unhealthy thought patterns and self-beliefs and yet still be perfectly sane. In fact, everyone has unhealthy thoughts and self-beliefs. The fact you have some insecurities and self-defeating mental habits is a sign that you are a normal human being.

But poor thought habits can actually cause some mental illnesses, such as anxiety or depression. It makes sense that thinking in harmful ways can take a toll on your psyche. As you think self-defeating thoughts and see their havoc on your life, it is easy to develop depression and anxiety as a response to these thoughts.

Self-induced mind control can help you overcome depression and anxiety as you fix your thought patterns. You stop thinking distressing thoughts and replace them with healthy, positive thoughts. The chemicals in your brain begin to balance. You have enough mental control to cope with your symptoms and cancel bothersome thoughts.

In addition, if you do have a mental illness, self-induced mind control can help you learn to manage your symptoms. You will have enough control over your mind to harness your thoughts and redirect them into more healthy ones. Self-induced mind control is not necessarily a cure-all for mental illness. You should not just go off of medication or quit therapy when you think you have mastered your mind. But it is a useful tool in managing and lessening symptoms. Perhaps in time you can wean off of meds and therapy if you achieve great enough mind control and success in life. Be sure to only do this with the advice and supervision of a qualified doctor, however. Quitting medication the wrong way can be harmful to your health and detrimental to the success of your self-induced mind control journey.

Chapter 6: The Challenges

In this chapter, I will cover some of the main challenges that you may face while learning self-induced mind control and how to overcome them. As I have mentioned before, this journey is not necessarily a stroll in the park. Rather, it can be like a hike up Mount Everest. But just as completing a challenging hike can feel empowering and rewarding, so can completing this journey. You must accept that there will be some challenges and then you must do your best to overcome them.

Losing People in Your Life

Part of self-induced mind control is gaining clarity about your life. Another part is building self-esteem. Unfortunately (or rather fortunately), this can reveal some people in your life to be very toxic.

People tend to attract like people. So if you have low self-esteem, you likely attract others with low self-esteem who feel better by being around you and dragging you down. If you do drugs or overeat or have some other vice, you likely surround yourself with friends who share your vices. You relate to people in the same boat as you and so you bond and find it easier to spend time together.

When changing your life, you begin to see that some of these people are really just holding you back. Usually they don't even intend to. They are just continuing habits that you no longer want to be a part of. When they see you try to better yourself, they fill you with doubt and negativity so that you cannot accomplish something that they feel is unattainable for themselves.

As you begin to change your life and gain control of your mind, you may find that you cannot relate to these people anymore. You may also find that they are actually holding you back, hindering your progress. That is not OK. There is no need to keep these people in your life, no matter how sentimental your relationship may be.

You may also find that they are resentful of you changing and letting them go. You may hear things like, "You have become so selfish," or "I don't even know you anymore! You have changed into someone I can't even recognize."

Don't let them manipulate you into feeling that your journey is selfish or that you are not changing into a better person. They can only see what is inside themselves; we all see the world through our own tinted glasses. If they are ugly inside or in an ugly place in life, then they will only see the changes you are making in an ugly light. That does not mean that you are changing for the worst. While you may be acting a little selfish, that is necessary to become a better person. You cannot let friends use these tactics to hold you back anymore.

Uncovering Unpleasant Facts about Yourself

Understanding your mind intimately is the backbone of self-induced mind control. You cannot control your thoughts if there are parts of you that you are repressing or denying. Those parts of you will simply bubble up eventually, making their presences known. Repression can manifest in many terrible ways, including in your subconscious thought patterns, which in turn can sully your progress in the direction of positive thinking and life change.

But there's a reason people repress things. From memories to dark aspects of their personalities, people only repress things to protect themselves. They wouldn't go through the rather lengthy process of repressing things if those things are pleasant and easy to accept.

Repression in itself is a form of mind control. You subconsciously or even consciously choose not to acknowledge an aspect of your life or of yourself. But repression is not healthy mind control. By repressing a part of yourself, you are creating a rift in your personality. Not everything in your mind adds up if a whole part of your mind is forcefully hidden away. Therefore, what you repress will begin to manifest. You may begin to have nightmares or flashbacks to a traumatic event that you are repressing, or you may begin to feel paranoid, as if your dirty secrets might end up out in the open.

Self-induced mind control will unearth all of the things that you are repressing. Gaining a true knowledge of your mind opens up every part of it, including the parts that you may not be so eager to explore.

You may encounter moments where you do not like things you are uncovering about yourself. Memories of things that you have done or that have happened to you. Thoughts you don't like to think. You may even begin to doubt your worth as a person when you have so much ugliness inside.

That's actually OK. You may think I'm crazy for saying that, but it's true. None of us are all peaches and cream. Many of us have dark, even evil, thoughts. Many of us have done terrible things in the past, or at least wanted to. Many of us have been the unfortunate victims of other people for no good reason at all, and many of us feel guilty for what others have wrongly done to us.

Nothing that you find out about yourself makes you truly evil or unworthy of betterment. The very fact that you want to overcome your life problems suggests that you are actually a good person, in search of a better life and a better self.

It is time to unearth what you are repressing and face it head-on. You have to face everything within your mind to get the proper control over it and to enjoy a better life in which you are in control. Do not let your repressed memories and personality facets destroy you or overwhelm you. This whole process is simply part of getting to know yourself really well, better than you have ever known yourself really.

Keep in mind that for all the bad things, there are a million good things you can uncover about yourself as well. You are not a bad person. Everything within you is uniquely you. Your scars, your thoughts, your fantasies, your dreams, your insecurities. Embrace everything, even if it hurts.

For help getting through the trauma of some repressed memories, consider counseling, a journal, or even just the confidence of a good friend. Read on for some ideas on overcoming this challenge.

Slipping Up

Self-induced mind control is a process. Sometimes throughout the process, you make great progress and think that you have finally attained mind control. Then, suddenly, you find your old bad thought patterns sneaking through again. Familiar worries, self-defeating thoughts, and negativity reappear in your mind, often sneakily. Your life begins to reflect this and things go south. Suddenly, you question if you really had control, and if you can ever get what little control you had back.

This can be stressful and downright disheartening. But it is all part of the process! This just indicates that you are getting the hang of self-induced mind control, but you are not 100% there. You just need to keep working at it and never give up.

Counseling?

Counseling can be a great option to help you in this journey.

Many people have a stigma against counselors. They think that counselors are only for crazy people. But going to a counselor does not mean that you are crazy or have a mental illness. It is true that counselors belong to the mental health profession, which does deal with "crazy" people. However, counselors are not necessarily for mental illness. Rather, they are there to help patients talk through their struggles and they can help patients retrain their minds to reject harmful thought patterns and self-beliefs.

You may find a counselor is helpful in identifying what thoughts and beliefs are hindering you. A counselor may also be able to help you discover where these beliefs stem from, such as events in your childhood. He or she can also teach you new, healthier ways of thinking about yourself and your life. When the challenges of self-induced mind control such as loneliness get to you, a counselor can provide you with a useful support system.

If you feel uncomfortable about seeing a counselor, that's perfectly OK. Counseling is not crucial. But if you begin running into confusion or if you become depressed about your journey and/or some of the repressed memories that you uncover, reconsider adding a counselor as part of your support network.

Support Network

Sometimes achieving self-induced mind control can be a lonely journey. As you get to know yourself, you don't have as much time for others. You lose friends and people that were once major in your life.

Really, this journey requires some alone time. It requires you to focus on yourself and even be a little bit selfish. That's OK. It's necessary. In the long run, you will be a better person to those around you if you dedicate some time to getting to know yourself and getting control over your own mind.

But being totally alone through such a hard journey is not advisable. Loneliness can deter you from pursuing this path. You can also become your worst enemy as opposed to your best friend.

That's why it is beneficial to form a support network of some kind. Your network is a group of positive people that encourage you on your journey and understand at least some of what you are going through.

Numerous people can be a part of your support network. Whoever makes you feel encouraged can be a part of it. Pastors, counselors, professors, co-workers, gym buddies, personal trainers, good friends, family members – there is no limit. It's also perfectly OK if there is just one solitary person in your support network. This is not a popularity contest. It is incredibly difficult to find people who actually support you. So even just one person that supports you in a positive way is sufficient.

If you are recovering from a trauma or vice, consider a support group. There are groups for trauma survivors, grieving victims of loss, and addicts of all kinds. These groups can be attended in person or online. They can offer tremendous help or they can hold you back by exposing you to negativity that you want to avoid. You will never know until you try it. Try a group out to see if it offers the support you need. You can always stop going if you don't like it.

Not everyone in your group needs to be friends with each other. You can have a support network that is spread out across many groups of people that do not know each other. Also, people in your group can be complete strangers, even to you. It is possible for them to not even be aware that they are in your support network. You could even consider a college class as part of your support network, if that class is helping you achieve a goal. As long as the people in your group make you feel empowered and positive, then they are supporting you. They don't have to be close friends and family who are in on your process of self-transformation.

Also, don't expect everyone in your support network to support you 100%, in every angle of your journey. You don't even need to tell members of your network that you are trying to achieve "self-induced mind control." Just involve these people in aspects of your positive transformation where they can truly help you. A personal trainer, for instance, may know that you are trying to get fit and lose weight. He or she can be involved in supporting you on that leg of your journey. There is no need to also involve him or her in your mental process, especially if he or she is a complete stranger.

The important thing is, is to keep your support network supportive. This means that toxic people cannot be a part of it. Rely only on those that make you feel better and help you attain your goals. If some person in your network starts to get nasty and nonconductive to your goals in any way, don't feel bad about cutting that person out of the network.

No matter what, remember that your #1 supporter is you. Don't rely on others too heavily. Other people have their own problems and unfortunately cannot understand you or make enough time to truly help you with every part of this long and complex journey into your own mind. Only you can really know yourself and only you can really control your mind. Make this journey about you, even if it is lonely, and don't rely too heavily on outside support for this internal mental undertaking.

Journaling

A journal is a super useful tool in this journey. It helps you get to know yourself and your innermost thoughts. It can also help you make sense of the sometimes confusing process of regulating your thoughts.

Consider a journal as another friend in your support network. The cool thing is, this friend is at your mercy. It is a true reflection of you. You confide everything in it, and never be betrayed or judged by anyone but your own self. You can make it do and say whatever you want to. Why not make it say nice things? Repeat positive mantras in it and use it to train your mind.

Focus on the Positive

When the dark parts of this journey hit, it is important to focus on the positive. This is part of training your mind. Focusing on the positive when the going gets rough is actually a real-life application of the theory provided in this book about how to train your mind and gain mind control.

Human beings have a natural tendency to focus more on the negative. Negative facts and opinions stick out at people far more than positive ones. Consumers can read fifteen positive reviews, but change their minds after reading a single negative one. People can see a person smile every day, but when they hear that he or she is rude, they are more likely to watch for rude characteristics and believe the bad. The bad things in this journey may stick out to you with alarming profundity, but do not dwell on them. They have no more import than the good things that are happening as well.

Even when the going is hard, remember to think of the positive things in your life and the positive changes that are occurring around you and within you. Keep a list of the good things in your life. Write down new skills you learn, positive improvements you have made, and things that you are grateful for. Just writing this list can release dopamine and serotonin in your brain, making you feel better. Use these lists as reminders that you are actually moving forward and doing well when you start to feel buried by the negativity.

Earlier I covered repression. One of the best things that you can do for yourself when you begin to get to know yourself, is to focus on the good and positive aspects of who you are. You are not all bad. For every bad thing you find out about yourself, there are countless good things. Don't fall into the tendency of overemphasizing the bad things about yourself; the bad things are not huger than the good. Again, a list can help. Write down the positive things about yourself. Write down what you do well. Maybe you are vindictive, but are you also a good listener with a caring personality?

The negative things you learn about yourself simply serve as a canvas for what you can improve about yourself. If you don't like something, change it. Even if you don't know how yet, part of the purpose of self-induced mind control is helping you learn how to change

yourself for the better.

Chapter 7: How It Works

A lot of people dismiss ideas like mind control, hypnosis, and meditation as New Age hocus pocus. Believe it or not, the success of these mental techniques actually are backed by real scientific evidence. They really do work! And there are solid scientific reasons why.

Meditation has long been observed as a useful method to attain relaxation and inner peace. But recently, mindfulness meditation has been found to have numerous benefits on pain management, PTSD treatment, and improving the quality of life for patients with chronic illnesses, such as cancer. Meditation lets you get in tune with your own mind and gain control over your thoughts and emotions for a little while. With that control, you are able to block out or reason through suffering, even of physical symptoms.

Basically, self-induced mind control is the ability to exist in a state of awareness like what you achieve with meditation. However, it is not practical to constantly be meditating. That interferes with your day-to-day life. Being able to be conscious, aware, and functioning at work, with family, while running errands, etc., and still being in tune with the inner workings of your mind is what self-induced mind control is all about.

What is so fascinating is that self-induced mind control is not like *The Secret*, where you just tap into the strength of the universe and magically everything you want is yours. This is not knocking *The Secret; The Secret* offers many valid points. However, there is a far more common-sense and tangible explanation for why self-induced mind control lets you attain what you want.

There is an example in *The Secret* that seems especially fantastic. The example involves a diamond necklace. You see the necklace in a store window, and you manifest that it is yours. You imagine yourself wearing it, touching it, opening up the jewelry box and running your fingers over it. Repeat the mantra that "This necklace is mine." Doing this consistently will make the necklace yours.

The practicality of this may be a bit of a stretch. Or it may not be. But it illustrates the simple concept that what you set your mind on is yours. Your mind has an amazing amount of control over you, even in ways that you do not realize or understand.

The mind is surprisingly powerful. Even your slightest emotions and most subconscious thoughts can manifest in your outer actions. That, in turn, shapes how you approach the world, and how people see you. If your inner thoughts are self-defeating, then without even realizing it, you are approaching the world in a self-defeating way. As a result, you will never succeed. Your mind is basically influencing you to set yourself up for failure.

Approaching life with the attitude that life and other people owe you something is equally detrimental to your success. Unfortunately, many people fall into the trap of believing this. If you believe it, don't feel like a bad person. But understand that your attitude is severely holding you back. Life does not owe you a thing; and if it does, well, life is rather poor at paying back its debts. You can go your whole life waiting for the things you want to be given to you and you will die in disappointment. Your attitude is preventing you from going after what you want and taking it for yourself.

Conversely, approaching life with an attitude of success can generate success for you. This isn't magic. This is you acting the way you need to act to get what you want. Believing that you can do it is essential to having the courage to do what you need to do.

Your attitude can make or break you when it comes to your goals. Even if your goal is a diamond necklace that seems unaffordable, actually believing that you can one day buy it can make it happen. The methods listed in *The Secret* are really just a crude form of self-induced mind control, where you condition your mind to be open to achieving your goals. This isn't the magic of the universe filling you and giving you what you want; instead, it is you taking charge and making your goals reality.

The idea that self-induced mind control can put you in charge of your fate is an empowering one. It is a much more comforting thought than the thought of relying on the elusive magic of the universe, which, let's face it, is never very giving or reliable. The universe may have power, but the strongest power is in your mind. Unleashing that power is the key to transforming your life.

Part of the reason for success with self-induced mind control is that you are setting goals. Once your goals are clear in your mind, you can begin to undertake them. According to Osman Abraham, goals give you focus. With focus, you can begin to think about how to achieve them. With that in your mind, you can begin to take steps, even just baby steps, toward them. Goals also give you a sense of purpose and a reason to move forward. They give you something to work toward.

Another part of the success of self-induced mind control lies in the fact that you are getting to know yourself. With healthy self-knowledge, you know that you are worth it. You also are able to think of realistic ways to attain your goals. Instead of deluding yourself with unrealistic expectations that set you up for failure, you are embracing who you really are and the ways you truly function. That way, you can make plans that actually work for you. You can corrode away your self-defeating beliefs that manifest in failure in your life, and instead begin actually taking active steps toward goal completion.

This is one of the things that separate truly successful people from "ordinary" people. It's not that some people are better than others. Just some people are better able to control their minds and thus their success. There are a plethora of articles out there about the differences between successful and unsuccessful people, but almost all of these articles point to a few key things:

1. Taking charge
2. Being joyful
3. Not blaming others for your failures
4. Not relying on others for your success

These are all things that lie at the core of self-induced mind control. Self-induced mind control results in you relying on yourself. But you are never too proud to refuse healthy support from others to get to where you need to go. You are taking charge of yourself and your life. Changing self-defeating beliefs and thoughts can make you more joyful. All of these things combine to make you ripe for success.

Another scientifically solid aspect of self-induced mind control's success is the way it alters your mind. Changing your thoughts to be more positive can help balance the neuro-chemicals in your brain. With a proper balance of chemicals, you feel better, and so you act better. You smile more and are more social. This attracts people to want to help you and follow your lead. This also attracts more positive people. Toxic people will no longer fit into your life and will fall away.

Many believe that the inner conscious is full of wisdom about how to live life. This wisdom has been collected throughout your years on earth. It is good wisdom, full of truth. But you may block out some of it. You may not be living to your full potential because you feel that you cannot. This is the result of mental blocks. Removing these blocks can open you to the knowledge your mind already stores about how to live life for optimal success. Self-induced mind control does not have you tap into some universal collective wisdom, but rather into your own wisdom.

It should be clear by now that self-induced mind control is all about self-empowerment. Everything you are capable of is within you. Even your failure is within you. That can be discouraging, until you understand that this means that you can turn your failure around into success. Self-induced mind control lets you on the real secret: that all power and wisdom for a better life lies within you, you just have to access it.

Chapter 8: Parting Thoughts

It is now time for this book to end, and for you to begin exploring self-induced mind control yourself. This is not a time to be sad. This is actually a very exciting opportunity and an exhilarating place to finally be in life. With this book and your own research and exploration, you now have the ability to take total control of your mind. That control gives you control of your life.

There is really nothing stopping you but your own thoughts and beliefs. That's what is holding you back from the life of your dreams. Your goals keep slipping away and your dreams keep dying because you do not have the mental setup to believe in yourself and take the proper action toward what you want. As a result, you feel as if your life is worthless and you keep screwing up.

This isn't true at all. These self-defeating beliefs are just that, beliefs. Beliefs can be altered. With the help of this book, hopefully you have pinpointed some beliefs that are holding you back. Now work on changing them. Change your own mind and your internal belief system into something that elevates you and propels you forward, rather than holding you back and hindering your progress. Change your thought patterns from those that hurt you, to those that make you feel good.

This book has hopefully given you some useful pointers on how to change your mental state. But hopefully it also gave you a sense of deserving, an attitude of being able and being good enough to effect the changes you need to do well in life.

Change is never easy. Sadly, this is just a fact of life. Like all habits, thought habits can be incredibly challenging to overcome. Adapting your lifestyle to one that is better for your new mental approach and your goals is also difficult, as you must lose certain friends and bad influences, and break certain old habits.

But if you are serious about your goals, then this change is far from too much. It is worth every little bit of struggle. As you train your mind to be yours, rather than your master, you begin to see your life change in ways that you are OK with. You begin to not obsess over the little things or mourn the death of bad relationships and bad habits. That's because you are finally ready to embrace a new life and you begin to see what is best for you.

If you ever have doubts, come back to this book for encouragement. You can also find online forums and groups of people dedicated to self-induced mind control where perhaps you can find support for your special situation. No matter what, don't give up. It is time for you to transform your life. No longer should you stay in the same old situation that made you feel terrible in the past. It never worked for you before; it won't work for you in the future. Change is what you need. And only you can make this change. So even if it gets lonely or confusing or hard, never give up.

No one can possibly understand how this journey has been for you. It may be hard, it may be triumphant. That's OK. That means that the triumph and satisfaction of overcoming your life challenges is all yours. You will be in total control, of your mind and of your success. That is a wonderful feeling.

I wish you the best the in this journey of mind control.

Thanks for reading!

Sources

Abraham, Osman. *Five Powerful Reasons Why Goal Setting is Important*. Code of Living. Web. June, 2016. Available from http://www.codeofliving.com/goals/5-powerful-reasons-why-goal-setting-important.

Byme, Rhonda. *The Secret*. Simon & Schuster: New York, NY. 2006. Print.

Palahniuk, Chuck. *Fight Club*. W.W. Norton: New York, NY. 1996. Print.

www.ingramcontent.com/pod-product-compliance
Lightning Source LLC
Chambersburg PA
CBHW050410290526
45786CB00003B/1203